THE LONG AND SHORT OF IT

Poems by

DAVID CONNOR

BLUE LIGHT PRESS

THE LONG AND SHORT OF IT

Copyright © 2015 by David Connor

BLUE LIGHT PRESS
www.bluelightpress.com
Email: bluelightpress@aol.com

BOOK DESIGN AND ILLUSTRATIONS
Melanie Gendron

COVER ART
"Crashing Waves" by Melanie Gendron

FIRST EDITION

Library of Congress Catalog Card Number: 2014921163

ISBN 9781421886947

TABLE OF CONTENTS

1. THE ARCHAEOLOGIST

2. SNOW ANGEL

3. WHAT THE THUNDER SAID

4. PHOENIX

5. THE LONG AND SHORT OF IT

THE ARCHAEOLOGIST

NIGHT

In my dream I was awakened
by noise from the alley below my window
at the Super 8 Motel.

Late night at the Eureka Super 8,
overlooking the alley which dead-ends
at the Launderland Wash and Dry,
drama was enjoying an encore.
The laundry, open 24 hours a day,
a natural collecting place for the homeless
to dry clothes and be dried out.

Beneath my balcony, police lights flashing,
two uniformed brutes noisily having trouble
convincing a scantily dressed young woman
that jabbing them with a four inch spiky heel
wouldn't get her sober or prevent jail time.

Lighted corners attracted hopeful creatures
slowly moving, hooded and homeless,
but now awake, prowling and searching
for the unexpected handout from a tourist.

The lingering odor of small arms recently shot
climbing up the back wall of an indoor range,
comingling with Italian scented garbage,
leftovers from Antonio's Diner next door.

My room was stuffy, so I opened the window
and let the senses of night lull me to sleep.

ESTATE SALE

*"Senator Ted Kennedy died in his prime from
a glioblastoma, a deadly brain malignancy.
If this were my diagnosis, I would have an estate sale."*
                              —David Connor, M.D.

If anyone out there is listening,
come to my estate sale.
I have gifts I was freely given;
I'm told I won't need them anymore.

If you are mother and child
on dialysis three times a week
from inherited Polycystic disease,
I have a kidney for each of you
which will soften guilt and betrayal.

If Hepatitis C found its way into hepatocytes,
plugging the exit of bile, and you are yellow,
starving and excoriating your skin,
I have a liver which can be shared by two.

Done with C-Pap, done with inhalers,
sorry you smoked for 100 pack years?
Have a lung of mine, share the other
with a brother on the chronic vent ward.

For the young diabetic so tired
of injections and glucose shifts,
my pancreas and its bed are yours
so the next 50 years will be easier.

I have an O-negative four-valved pump
for someone with a failed heart.
Right before they start the fentanyl drip,
lay down next to me, bare your chest.
The incisions are long but heal side to side.

Transfer my remaining skin to the burn unit,
layer it onto all who need a covering.
If it's the pediatric ward, I'll service many more.

Examine my brain with fancy gadgets
and compare it to the results
of all the Minnesota Multiphasic Personality Inventories
I was forced to take over the years.

The rest you can incinerate and scatter to the sea;
my soul has already flown away.

CLOSURE

I will not travel to see the endangered
Turquoise-Browed Motmot
in the Rincon Volcano Forest
of Costa Rica, so I won't need
to find closure on that species.

I've seen leopards and giraffes,
and now I've visited my Uncle Dean
in Woodbury, Minnesota.
I've seen him each year
at the Wahlberg family reunion,
except for the years we served
the country in different wars.

I have recently attended for the last time
Class Reunions of 50 and 55 years
of my college and high school.
I will not pass under a banner
welcoming me back to an alma mater
as the last survivor of the class.

I said goodbye to old chums and girlfriends,
to the two houses where I grew up,
and to Pershing Field where I learned to skate.
I missed John and Jerry who died
before they made closure with me.
One classmate has post-polio syndrome,
another at the end of pancreatic cancer,
and I said goodbye to them.

On Sunday morning I walked to church,
Mt. Olivet Lutheran on 50th and Knox.
I was confirmed there in 8th grade
and sang "God of our Fathers" for the last time.
The ceremony has varied little in 63 years,
serving 2000 members in 4 Sunday shifts.
Once Pastor Reuben Youngdahl placed a button
instead of a Smith Brothers cough drop in his mouth,
so the sermon ran beyond its usual 12 minutes.

The *Minneapolis Star Tribune*
reported that 84% of bridges
built in this country since 1960
were unsafe, cracked and crumbling —
even the Brooklyn Bridge was beyond its prime.
If they all fall down at once,
we will have nowhere to go but here
until we learn to fly without planes
like the birds of the tropical jungles.

DOGS GET BORED, TOO

When my two Bichons Frises females
get that vague feeling of discontent,
they give me "the look" which says,
"We're bored locked in the house all day."
I do what we both want — I take them for a walk.

Bella is bored when her dog dish is empty.
Bitsie is a birder and wants to find sparrows.
I get bored every hour or two and need to get out.

None of us drink alcohol or watch TV,
common remedies for boredom
in the American human race.
We want fresh air, a change of scene
and chances to mingle our scents with others.

Ivan Denisovich was bored every day
in the deep chill of the Gulag.
e. e. cummings had little to do
with prisoners in the Enormous Room.
I can't imagine the Elms was a beehive of activity,
and James Russell Lowell just wrote.

Samuel Taylor Coleridge stayed indoors,
dozing stoned, dreaming of mariner rimes.
W.B. Yeats played with wattles and clay.
Herman Melville sailed the South China Sea,
chasing sperm whales and repairing sails.
Obviously, none of these poets had dogs.

When recent presidents had time on their hands
and no major international crises to handle,
they took solace in ways to amuse themselves.
Nixon took Haldeman's advice and percodan.
Clinton whistled and Monica flashed her silver thong.
Grant rode to the officer's tent for bourbon,
and Eisenhower called for his driver.

When I'm bored, I call my dogs,
pick a path under shady maples
and let them take me for a walk.

LOSING IT

"The art of losing isn't hard to master."
—*Elizabeth Bishop*

If I lose car keys, I try to remember
when I last had them in my hand.
I go on the offensive, sit down,
recall when something wasn't
where it should have been from habit.

Like love, for instance.
I loved my Lone Ranger pedometer,
having sent my 25 cents to Nabisco.
When it came in the mail, I didn't dare tell Mom!
It wouldn't have been about 25 cents
but about the purpose of the purchase —
what with children starving in China
and, "What if you lose it?"

Which I soon did: off my belt,
down cinder blocks stacked
for porch steps at a new house
covered with cement the next day.

As I grew, I lost things never recovered:
my blue Superman sweatshirt,
the Timex wrist watch from Aunt Fran,
the Omega watch from Grandma Connor,
a switchblade the night I saw *Rebel without a Cause*,
a plaque awarded by the Captain of the USS Barry.

I lose track of the days in the week,
the times in the day
and forget moments of extreme importance
or the emotions I felt.
I lost the feeling of panic I had once when drowning.

I have lost parents, a wife, 2 children and 3 dogs.
Someday, I'm going to lose my dread of getting older
but not the promise I made
to make certain I offend visitors at my funeral
when I'm the one finally lost forever.

THE ARCHAEOLOGIST

Raccoons, silent thieves of night,
overturned my neighbor's garbage can,
left the site littered with savory remains
collected for this week's trash.
Archaeologists are trained to dig
through discards from the past,
to pick and probe into years of waste,
treasuring what others have left behind.

I was Carter entering Tut's tomb,
first to breathe the musty air
from a desiccated Pharaoh.

"What do you see?"

"Wonderful things."

The couple next door to our house in Marin
are a secretive pair, seldom around.
They left a rich smorgasbord
spread out for critters and nosy folks.
Several items, not preserved, were
meant for weekly removal.
In my process of returning the spoils
to their rightful plastic container,
I found several things of interest:

Six wine bottles, all drained.
Corks from bark of Portuguese trees.
A broken serving spoon, gravy stained,
two old plates, chipped and useless.
Medicine cabinet discards:

Penicillin for the flu, Oxycontin for pain,
Nytol for sleep, Repose for nerves,
Dr. Scholl's solution for sore feet,
Pepto-Bismo for a distasteful omelet.

A tattered copy of *Portnoy's Complaint*,
a ketchup bottle one quarter filled,
turkey bones, (I could tell by the femur),
a fish head from a rainbow trout.

Next to flattened cans of Coors,
an old tarnished necklace.
Surprised to find dental floss,
certain King Tut had no teeth.
A hair brush with black curly strands,
though both neighbors are grey.
An airline stub for Arizona,
golf score card from La Quinta.
A leather strap, certainly usable,
until I remembered they had horses.
Two pairs of children's shoes,
well worn from skate-boarding.

I secured the garbage can lid
the way Carter sealed the tomb
of the boy king, so raccoons
and grave-robbers would leave unspoiled
treasures within.

DREAMING THE COLORS OF MUSIC

"Our dreams wrestle in the castle of doubt
but there's music in us."
                                    —Jack Gilbert

I do not see colors.
Contained in my DNA
is a sex-linked recessive gene,
a gift from Mom.

My red and blue striped shirt
didn't match bright orange corduroy pants.
I couldn't color between the lines.
I flunked signage at the DMV
and was rejected by the Air Force.

I wonder if colors make sounds?
I couldn't see autumn's changing leaves
but could hear them crackling in the wind.
One night my dreams led me
to an amusement park with a splashy display
of rainbows and fireworks on the Fourth of July.
I saw those colors for the first time
and heard an orchestra playing behind a curtain.

I listened to yellow trombones
leading the brass
and blue trumpets blaring at the bar.
Black notes from bass fiddles
danced the pizzicato of a minor chord
as the conductor was keeping time
in a purple sequined robe festooned with silver flowers.
I saw rose colored notes float over the golden harp
and forest green blasts from French horns.

Seeing colors mixed with sounds in my dreams
gave me new energy to enjoy what I was missing
while picturing the world in black and white.

Beethoven had Paget's Disease,
his listening compromised,
but he had an inner hearing for music.
As he conducted his Ninth Symphony,
he could sense delicious and colorful
melodies rising from strings and voices.

PICKING UP DOGS

Dogs don't get a vote or swear on the Bible.
No trial offered, no lawyer, no judge.
Theirs is the hasty withdrawal from court to jail,
unknown sentence, no bond, no bail.

My Bichons Frises were caged in a dungeon —
little light, strange shadows, foul air,
surrounded by prisoners.

None of the dogs were guilty,
no stolen food, no spots on rugs.
Everything pointed to humans
packing suitcases for vacations.

One owner deposited
dogs at the front polished desk
below a sign saying: "Klean Kennel" —
a travesty on reality but a necessity
as husband and wife had separate agendas.

She had to bring them there.
The other owner, fishing trout streams
in the redwoods, shortened forest time,
headed south to end their internment.

I am protective of furry creatures
orphaned to join the human world.
Despite a brisk southerly wind,
they were stuck in the doldrums,
and I felt a strong urge to rescue them.

My little dogs, Bitsie and Bella,
were cuddling and grasping each other
while sprawled on the moldy floor
beside stagnant polluted water.

Back in my company I was treated
to moans and yelps and licks and looks
and felt adored as The Savior who is seated
at the Right Hand of God.

GRINDSTONE LAKE CHRISTMAS, 1920

On Christmas Eve, Father Bert, with axe in hand,
cut the large spruce nearest the house,
so fresh that adorned with lighted candles
nothing burned up or down.

In 1920, my Mother was a child of 5.
She had 2 brothers and 4 sisters.
Leonard, Clara and Arnold were older;
Esther, Norma younger than Helen
but all under 10, and she was number 4.
Father was 50 and Mother Lil, 36.
They all lived together
in a square 4 room farmhouse.

No stockings were hung
as there was no chimney.
No gifts exchanged
as there was no money.
No seasonal cheer lifted
as they were teetotalers,
and no Santa or reindeer,
as this was the Birth of Jesus.

After the morning milking
the family gathered for breakfast.
Eggs and potatoes and buns
but no bacon, as remains of the pig
slaughtered in August were gone.

A younger child might get an orange
or an extra piece of apple pie.
The youngest girl, Norma, was special;
she wore the candle-lit crown of St. Lucia
and woke everyone up with warm *krumkaka*.

No matter how much snow or cold,
the team of horses was hitched
and drove the sleigh to church,
where all sang Swedish hymns.

Four boys came later.
Bert had his farm hands,
but they matured during two wars,
left the land and served their nation,
so there wasn't much joy at Christmas.

Electricity didn't come to the farm
for another 25 years. Cows quit milking
and chickens quit laying until
they all got used to lights and radio.

Lights preceded indoor plumbing,
which was finally installed in 1955,
but on the day Grandfather finished,
he fell off the ladder, broke his neck
and died, leaving the milking to Lil.

RISE AND SHINE YOGA

*"Between the sheer rock of Scylla
and the whirlpool of Charybdis
the sea forever spouted and roared."*
                    —*Jason and the Argonauts*

Rise and Shine Yoga
with Julie Karsky began the day.
As we lumbered through
the twelve positions
of the Sunrise Salutations,
she challenged us:
"transport yourself
to a mythological place,
to see this world around you."

To follow Julie's journey to meditate,
I traveled from Center City, Minnesota
two miles from Chisago Lake,
through the narrow straits of
Scylla and Charybdis in the Sea of Marmara.
Sucked into the endless whirlpool,
I suited up with scuba gear
and slid into the abyss of Charybdis
that whirled around me,
feeling like Jason and Odysseus
on their famous expeditions.
I controlled my descent
as if I were in the Bahamas
and was alarmed by what I saw.

The *London Times* from April 22, 1912
flashed by shouting the tragedy
of the great ship Titanic sinking.
Since this newspaper hadn't arrived
at the locker of Davy Jones,
no vessels had been dispatched
to find the drowned.
I was soon surrounded by able-bodied seaman
spinning and desperately swimming
with tee-shirts showing their ship:
the USS Arizona, now a mile overhead.

I caught a glimpse of Robert Wagner
bent over the gunwale rails
watching Natalie Wood floating
like a piece of balsa,
wondering if she was ruining
her skimpy cocktail dress.
Stuck behind a water wagon
were several who had fallen off,
slouching and trudging happily
back to recovery in Center City .

When the meditation was over,
we ran barefoot over
the snow covered lawn,
saluting the sun rising through
the gray morning fog off the lake.

MOMENTS OF HAPPINESS

*"after the only conversation is
to enjoy your own happiness."*
—Diane Frank, "Floating Redwoods in the Early Morning"

Happy are moments with music:
the marching band at high school football games,
the Supremes' concert with a new date in college,
Mendelssohn's prelude before your wedding,
the hip-hop sweaty dance at the nuptial ball.

Joyful the sounds at anniversary or birthday parties:
off key singing to smooth jazz in a smoky bar,
moments of musical happiness which follow you home,
whistling about corn and elephants from Oklahoma.

Somewhere the key becomes
Beethoven's Third Symphony in E-Flat Major.
Smiles and cheers disappear,
and as the record slows and stops,
Blake's angels with harps appear.

MISERY

"We are not fond of misery."
—*Pablo Neruda: "Poverty" from The Captain's Verses*

My career as a physician was spent
attending to miseries of patients
inflicted with nephrologic disorders,
most of which were incurable.

I passed the burden on
to the next generation of medics
who still had patience and heart
to welcome the daily challenge.

I still hear misery but of a different type,
from the newly sober young adult
crawling from a pit of despair and poverty
into arms of early recovery, hoping
for a future starting today.

"If I only had a house and a car,
a job, and ten thousand dollars."
A tall order but a minor wish
for someone living in America.

There is misery as factory walls crumble in Bangladesh,
and Syrian troops spray civilians with poison.
Chinese peasants climb out of earthquakes
as the boardwalks in New Jersey
are battered by Great Storm Sandy.

If happiness is the absence of misery,
I'm happy.
If security is having health, hearth and wealth,
I'm secure.
If puppy love is a warm blanket,
I'm comforted.
If the aging process is as pleasant as mine,
I'm not concerned with time.

LOOKING WEST AT 3 P.M.

The sun is flying
on the surface of the bay
shining into the darkness
of shadows from the mountain.
Each reflected ripple
is a pulse of whispered life
growing from the funnel tube
into a cornucopia of overflowing relief.
I hear the twinkle from drops
falling off feathers as they vibrate,
strains of a lullaby
from the golden reflection
as it dives low into itself
at the far end
of sleep.

SNOW ANGEL

GUANO AT THE DOCTOR'S HOUSE

There must be a
chemical abnormality
in the brain of a mature
grasshopper sparrow
that compels it to fly round and round
a house with plate glass windows,
to peck at and poop on
consecutive window sills.

After each lap it
perches and preens
on a four foot juniper bush,
then flies again to worry
any clean window it sees,
mimicking a man or woman
in the cubicular office,
who must leave their space
to snoop at all the other desks
surviving the monotony of their jobs.

It's a natural curiosity
to peek between the branches
and check for new scat on the trail
or wonder what new beast
rubbed bare the bark of an elm.
If twigs are sighted in a mound
and pebbles gathered to a heap,
this may herald a new den
for a family of silver tailed foxes.

Dogs and cats mark their territory
with scented uriniferous sprays.
Humans place sidewalks and fences
on boundary lines, park cars in slots
and always use the front door,
ignoring the backyard barbeque next to
the statue of St. Francis with bird droppings.

A long ago relative of the bird
likely nested in a tree
that stood for a hundred years
in the exact spot now occupied
by the aviary stained house.

Our sparrow wants to enter
and live in that mystical tree
where ancient cave birds
nested and gathered and fed.
Going on the attack each day
is its method of replaying
happy memories of the virgin forest
with special trees for every flock.

AT THE REDWOOD CAFE

On stage a talented pair
bowing the cello
reading poems
playing to an attentive audience
in the front half
of the Redwood Cafe.

Two cowboys, necks red,
sat at a front table
nuzzled long-necks
and spoke to each other
as if their voices had to compete
with a thundering fleet
of wild mustang ponies.

They talked about chicken shit
surrounding their lives,
letting them wallow in thoughts
no higher than the sty.

They didn't know a cello
from a bass drum
nor an ode from an ovary,
a ballad from boots.

They must have been hatched
from a giant ostrich egg
much earlier than the yolk.
They never learned manners
and were now part of a joke.

The cellist gently strummed
his bow over their beers,
telling them they were louder
than all the folks in the back room.

They took the hint and moved outside
and scared away the pigeons.

SEWING CLASS

"A stitch in time saves nine"
—*Benjamin Franklin*

Count them all, line them up,
every 30 minutes, another batch
of toddlers who hadn't far to fall
are moved from chair to table
in every emergency room in the suburbs
from noon to 8:00 p.m. on sunny weekend days.

We expect them and tell by cries
that children are waiting
with split chins, gashed lips and scalps,
caused by gravity defying dives.

Each child is pried from grieving arms
to the hidden area behind curtains
where a nurse straps them onto a frame
the way old Nokomis used to carry Hiawatha.
Secured, squalls ignored, the new
doctor in training pricks the prepped skin
injects that which numbs and silences
and the sewing class begins.

Snap on size 8 gloves,
clamp the curved needle armed with silk,
and evenly suture edges together,
snip ends, cover the results
with a butterfly band-aid.

Fill the butt with tetanus toxoid
and send them back to Mom and Dad —
back to running with abandon,
back to trips on tricycles,
back to sudden falls,
back to the emergency room.

CONSIDER THE TRUTH

"Write the poem that can't be written."
—*Stephen Dunn*

The lowest rung of Dante's Inferno
contains the three most despised:
Judas, Cassius and Brutus.
They were the ones who betrayed
he who loved and trusted them.

Are there candidates still alive
who fit that description?
Even the monsters of the earth
didn't make the list in death.

Alive today are those who damage
those placed in their charge
with trust, faith and love
for that man or woman:

Doctors and nurses who willingly end patients' lives,
armed men of the military who kill their leaders in battle
and follow orders to slaughter civilians,
priests who damage altar boys and demand their silence,
presidents who threaten members of their constituency,
CEOs who cook the books and fake reports,
brokers who leak lies and sell short,
taxi drivers who rob their passengers,
teen-aged boys who spike the drinks of young dates
or massacre second graders,
mechanics who don't tighten the connections enough,
pharmaceutical managers who contaminate ingredients,

government contractors bribed to accept high bids,
morticians who keep gold fillings of their clients,
husbands and wives who cheat,
children who lie to and steal from their parents.

However, the worst offender
is the person who doesn't love and trust
the person he or she is.

VISITOR

The white moth
made a grand entry
into the kitchen and our lives
by colliding with an alabaster shade
and landing on a plate
of chili con carne
and grilled bok choy.

Six struggling legs
firmly grasped my finger.
It flew to my ear,
explored my hair,
climbed down my neck,
perched on my shoulder,
looking around for kitchen beetles.

The wings were grey speckled,
not dusty but full and moving,
eager to leave our party.
It flew to the lower lip
of a carved Aztec mask
and met the gecko.

Now we have an unlikely couple
in our midst while we dine:
the gecko playing Romeo
to a beckoning Juliet
fluttering on her balcony.

The lizard and the moth
decided to honeymoon
here in Mexico, on the beach.
They settled in a large fig tree
danced a salsa while we had coffee
and fired up cigars.

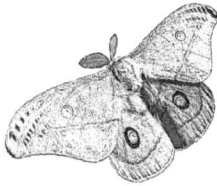

NIGHT IMAGES

"Take a breath, and enjoy receiving trillions of atoms
of oxygen — most of them the gifts of an exploding star."
—Rick Hanson, Buddha's Brain

Airways were filled with news
of an imminent surprise:
a total solar eclipse
would obliterate sunrise.

I hurried to Land's End
with the Golden Gate below,
equipped with shielding radiographs
to see and hear an eclipse sing.

I skipped my morning lithium,
didn't call my shrink,
pretended I took acid
and watched the sun disappear
into the shadowing moon.

In the darkness this morning,
I imagined seeing clusters of galaxies
shooting out aptly named nebulae
to sprinkle new suns into the void,
scattering hydrogen and helium
over a few oxygen molecules.
Stand back and watch
another Big Bang.

As the noise ebbed like the ocean around me,
I thought I heard Galileo speaking to Hubbard
in a cryptic tongue: "I was right."

The stars that dazzle us tonight
were extinguished 200 million light years ago,
but we on this speck, way out on the Milky Way,
still feel empowered by naming Orion.

Orion, keep chasing Taurus,
put a flint into the Pleiades.
Ask Sirius to stop nipping at Rigel
and turn your aim north
to strike the Great Bear,
who drags a dipper with his tail.

The Vikings followed stars
up the Red River to Alexandria, Minnesota
and left a stone engraved in rune characters:
"These red skinned natives are tough,
they slaughtered our boat keepers.
We're getting out of this place."

Now the starry night can whisper
memories to my soul as I hear
an eclipse sing.

SNOW ANGEL

"after one day, maybe next week
after ice storms wrapping trees"
—Diane Frank, *"Floating Redwoods in the Early Morning"*

Lie down, spread your arms and legs
look to Heaven and flutter your wings
until you've made an angel in the snow.

Driving south on the Interstate,
Highway 35E in Minnesota,
I couldn't see beyond my headlights
or even out my window covered with sleet,
created by the winter storm

First to fall, the icy sleet,
and following a drop in temperature,
giant floating snowflakes drifted down,
covering bare branches and boughs
of every tree lining the Mississippi
making a landscape of delicate sculptures.

Currier and Ives sent painters
as children scampered to play in the blizzard.
From fluffy drifts giant snowmen grew
and all bundled humans had a rosy nose.

Traffic stopped on land and air.
If you weren't already there,
you were here and not leaving.
Sleepy interns followed their 12 hour shifts
with another, and men driving plows
kept plowing to clear roads for the morning.
Everyone at home was snowbound.
"Children, we need dig a tunnel to the garage."

A perfect storm at sea will kill,
but on land it only chills.
Across the way 1000 Minnesotans
lined up and bundled up near Albert Lea.
On a signal they laid down on a corn field
and made 1000 perfect snow angels.

When climatic characteristics coalesce,
restore your angel to inner peace.

LOVE IN THE SOUL

*"I'd tell it as evidence of the strange places
the soul hides, and why I fell in love."*
—*Stephen Dunn, "Juarez"*

My parents were probably in love,
but I didn't feel heat from their bedroom.
Is there a connection between soul and love,
and do we have evidence that either exists?

My father, a traveling salesman,
was absent from family activities all week.
My mother, a Swedish housewife,
raised three children, opened doors at school,
was there for the kids when they tried,
tucked us in bed when we cried.

When first you meet a person,
you talk of love and may marry.
If realizing you have no love in your heart,
you turn to God, expose your soul;
"Is this it, God? Am I whole?"

When are we complete?
We were born with a soul, though we were all self
and develop the spirit traveling through life.
Along our path there may be love
at the tip of Cupid's arrow, or from comfort.

David loved Bathsheba; their children died sadly young.
Delilah felt strongly for Samson
but cut off his hair and his strength.
Cleopatra grasped whomever came by;
fondled the men and the final serpent.
Dido immolated herself as Aeneas sailed away.

Love if true replaces reason; lust will fade away.
The soul may be the meeting place
for love and God's direction.
Love is never having to say you're sorry,
but being human, I can be wrong.
Patton thought bullets, not love, would conquer.
"Love endureth all," said Paul.

Without love there would be no children,
but Mormans have solved that issue.
Love outside marriage may get you a Puritan A.
Love is driving 400 miles for a kiss, a silly waste of gas.
I tell my soul to be open for love
without requiring evidence.

ODE TO THE UNIVERSE

"You may live in one of two ways:
either nothing is a miracle or everything is a miracle."
                    —*Albert Einstein*

Having tracked the embryo's development
on its week-to-week parade
by 40 black and white glossies,
I found pictorial proof that a miracle occurred
whenever a sperm successfully
penetrated a waiting ovum.

Sockeye salmon spawning,
silver salamanders slithering,
solitary spiders spinning,
spotted hummingbirds sipping
nectar fresh from birds of paradise,
all seem miraculous to me.

I live, alas, in a world
of reality and sin. I try
to be my brother's keeper
but I frequently fail.

Darwin may have explained
the process of creation,
but when I see a star,
twinkling just for me,
I don't care it may have burned out
200 million light years ago.

Einstein, who never memorized,
has kept us all mesmerized
with universal and relative theories
that dealt with the mass of humans
and the mess they have made
of this earthly kingdom because
they didn't believe in miracles.

UNPLUGGED

Imagine electrons
whizzing around their nuclei,
wondering when someone
is going to turn the light on?

Is there a Congressional Committee
comissioned to halt sparkis interruptus?
Should we leave the lights on?

Those must be lively debates:
Southern Senators who have more sun,
Northern Senators who hate dark,
lobbyists from the entertainment biz
who need bright lights 24/7 for Reno,
environmentalists from Idaho
who love living in the dark?

Edison is the culprit; he invented the bulb.
Franklin is the maven; he discovered electricity.
Fermi and his crew invented nuclear fission
and light much brighter than the Hoover Dam produces.
The thing about fission — it takes more to start the flow
than fumbling in the dark for a light switch.

They didn't have florescent bulbs in Rome,
but it lit up as Nero fiddled.
If we ran around unplugging the world,
would universal peace reign?

THAT WAS A FIERY MINK

I understand why
mink coats are expensive.
Minks are small, hard to catch
and vicious at close quarters.

Early walking on the side of the road
from where I slept to Dillingham, Alaska,
ahead a furry hotdog-sized creature
hustled her family away from roadway threats.

What was a mink doing crossing the road?
That was an old chicken joke.
This mother was tending to business,
guiding her brood towards a pond.

I stopped on a knoll
sloping towards a grassy ditch
when the rustling of leaves
betrayed the hidden family.

Mom rose to her full 12 inches,
stood her ground, stared me down.
She hissed a menacing warning
to leave her family in peace.

I outweighed her 500-fold
and was 10 feet above her head,
but she never faltered or blinked.
I was the one who backed away.

INNER STRENGTH

*"An alphabet's molecules, tasting of
honey, iron, and salt . . ."*
　　　　　　　—Jane Hirschfield

A beehive run over by a train
moving swiftly near an ocean shore
will have a distinct taste
of honey, iron and salt.

Molecules of ink
fresh from the printer
though stuck to the page
are in constant motion.

Alphabet letters become a poem
when a series of words try to attach
end to end between engine and caboose
to make a lingering, lucky line.

Hopefully, they will taste of honey
like a stacked sonnet
or become a salty sestina
in a fish rag on an Atlantic City pier.

But a poem with vision and depth
will have an iron girder design,
and the language will blow off
a reader's head.

THE LAST VISTA

". . . one might find a vista like this,
perhaps, once in a lifetime . . ."
　　　　　　　—C. Dale Young

I stand on a bare mountain
dazzled by the design,
shadows broken by light
through the long passage.

I have flown through wrinkled boulders
of tightly stacked cumulus clouds.
Diving into the tongue of the ocean,
I felt the trench 6000 feet below.

Eliot, Pound and Yeats set Paris glowing,
and I felt that heat 50 years later.
I have stared in awe at blue-domed mosques,
Venetian canals, and the four horsemen on St. Marks,
gasped at Niagara Falls rushing,
applauded as Old Faithful gushed on time.

I admired swimming elephants
spraying over our safari boat
and plugged my ears in response
to a Saturn rocket pushing an Apollo
into the sky with its nervous crew.

I have a vista I'll see only once,
and that will be the last sunrise
on the day I die, before they suture my lids
and fill my veins with formaldehyde.

No one who has seen that vista
has ever returned to write about the view.
I suspect it is so amazing
they remain on the empty mountain
staring and sighing forever.

WHAT THE THUNDER SAID

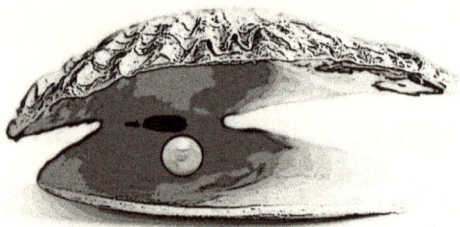

GLUTTONY

Oysters do not complain when
chewed and swallowed alive,
as they have no vocal cords.

On a long naval cruise
dulled by boredom, canned peaches
and meatloaf built around
three hard-boiled eggs,
I fantasized about eating
dozens of live oysters
at a wooden bar in Scully Square
on the Boston waterfront . . .

The Union Oyster House is old,
its wooden bar scarred with secrets
hidden in crevices of ancient eaves.
Pulling up a stool, elbows planted,
I receive plate after plate of 7 oysters
freshly shucked and accompanied
by chilled beer and salty crackers
until I say, "Stop!"

That night on shore
I solely and clearly devour
42 chilled mollusks.

In the restless dream that followed,
I was the patient etherized on the table
as the bearded surgeon sliced me from
my substernal notch to my symphysis pubis
and declared, "His stomach has ruptured.
He had one too many oysters, and now
they are slithering in his peritoneum."

My stomach was closed and I recovered,
but they only removed 41 parts of my recent dinner.
One oyster was still on the loose, sealed within me,
a lonesome traveler without a shell.

MASKED MAN

Wise Greek authors told tales
on stages through masks
so actors could show fear,
love and rage.

I am a creature of the dark.
I see shadows others miss.
I don't need a moon or a candle
to light my path, silently marked.

In the sunlight, I wear a mask
to be whoever you want me to be.
I read your eyes and play the role,
allowing you to breathe with ease.

Want to talk of tennis or golf,
scuba, bridge or fly fishing?
I can handle bocce or canasta
and discourse on medical woes.

I carry all my masks with me;
I'm never caught without disguise.
Give me a word and I will earn your trust
like a sly coyote at the chicken's door.

I needn't wear a mask
when driving alone.
I listen to philosophers
telling why masks are worn.

When in denial, show a mask of joy.
When unhappy, glare with an angry face.
If troubled, look puzzled,
and if you feel desire, add long eyelashes.

Naked in bed with a lover,
two on top of the sheets,
masks are not required to bare your soul,
and in the process, to become whole.

DYING YOUNG

"Where does Hitler sleep in Hell?
Perhaps, on barbed wire among
children's ashes, bitten for eternity
by black mastiffs under a cloud of gas."
—Pablo Neruda: The Book of Questions

Were Dante still listing
levels in the Inferno,
he would have to add cantos
for the Twentieth Century.

Social tides collide
spewing forth monsters.
Our planet is so crowded that as
terrestrial plates convulse,
whole populations are destroyed,
mimicking what famous monsters did.

Current medical literature is buzzing
with news of an aberrant immunoglobulin
discovered 10 years ago in Japan,
thought to have mutated
from environmental pollution.

This means that all we breathe and eat
develops an antibody rage
so complex and frightful, we scar
our organs from the inside out.

Our future may be no better than Hitler's,
as we will all end up on a heap of our ashes.

AT THE CENTER OF MY WORLD

"Where is the center of the sea?
Why do waves never go there?"

Put me down in the middle of the desert
near an oasis with palm trees, rather than
alone on an isolated sand dune without water.

Place me in the center of the ocean
where there is neither wind nor waves.
I will kick and thrust to make my own
and ride them playfully to shore.

The ocean rolls but waves rise
to reach foam-crowned height.
I will surf them with joy and freedom,
crash with force and thunder
to reclaim the ebbing shore.

Dolphins ride over waves,
salmon swim through them,
crabs crawl under them
and land always surrounds them.

Waves are the foamy fingers of God,
gently rearranging the line
established early in time
when all was water and whales.
Finally, plants and trees made shore,
pushing roots and branches into eternity.

Fierce storms ravage land,
but the sea settles them down
by sending endless sweeps of waves
to smooth the shoreline.

I trod the earth,
I swim the sea.
Both nourish me,
but waves set me free.

SHOULD I FEAR DEATH?

> *"At present you need to live the question;*
> *then you might, without noticing it, some day*
> *live the answer."*
> > *Letters to a Young Poet*
> > *—Rainer Maria Rilke*

I have seen the face of death
calmly claiming the ill beyond help.
I wonder how I will react when
my appointed time has come?

It doesn't hurt to die, in fact,
death often relieves pain
at a time when suffering
has endured too long.

As a physician, I was reminded
that filing and signing a form
for the coroner made
the recently deceased legally dead.

I have followed the rhythm strip
as the last recorded heart beat
was followed by an uninterrupted
straight line.

I have watched through an ophthalmoscope
the blood slowing in the retinal artery's branches
until the distinctive box-car appearance
of the red corpuscles stopped.

I have watched pupils dilate
when we ceased to ventilate
a brain-dead patient to hasten
the transfer of his organs.

I have been the last to hear
a victim of a 98% third degree burn
whispering in my ear before he died,
"please call my wife and a priest."

I witnessed a brakeman
coupled at midwaist between freight cars
and held his hand as the latch
holding two halves of his body together
was released.

I know our mission on earth will end
like a train striking a stranded bus.
We shouldn't fear that death.

GROUP SEX

Nudibranchs, sea hares and squid,
pick a moonless night
to roll around the ocean floor.
Sons and mothers,
clutched to each other,
produce more gill-less creatures.

Early morning, over California's Fall River,
mayflies congregate to copulate.
They form a flying ball so big and dense
you can't see the opposite shore.
The frenzy lasts for 30 minutes and stops
as the balloon of insects springs a leak
and deflates to cover the smooth surface.

The carpet of spent carcasses
is swept downstream by current.
How I can raise a rainbow trout
from the bottom, through the bodies,
using an artificial fly, is a mystery.

Over the river and up the hill,
cows line up and wait their turn
to be mounted and serviced
by a stud bull once a year.

In the mountains young male moose
prance and strut and show new racks
to adoring, waiting females.
These young studs are in their prime,
and with his place in the herd taken,
the defeated old bull stands and stares,
comforted only by last spring's memories.

ODE TO THE MOON

Moon, I know so little of your
orbit, rotation and wobble;
but I know you're not made blue
by curdled Swiss milk
or yellow by daisies in outer space.
I've trusted you since I first saw
your reflection off Lake Harriet,
as I was necking with a Minneapolis girl.

So unpredictable to a teen in love,
I tended to rhyme you with June.
I found you have a dark side,
though we see only the side that shines.
Your changing face is not from shadow
but from angles with the sun.

I, too, have a dark side
pockmarked like yours with obstacles.
Asteroids flew at you; mine snuck up on me.
I see them only fleetingly
while I'm confessing my shortcomings
to myself, to God, and to another human.

Were you bothered when astronauts
planted a flagpole through your skin,
drove around in crater buggies
collecting fragments for a museum?
Once they saluted the dark side of Earth,
they abandoned you to shine alone.

I remain on solid California ground,
ego driven with a list of faults.
I've been trained to produce and provide
wealth for family, health for patients,
and I want to be like you, steady in orbit,
present and comforting with many faces.

MY LIBRARY

This is the place I carved from dirt,
under the house, dry and cozy,
near howling wind and breaking waves.

Red-tailed hawks soar over my head.
Sea otters migrating too far north,
share the water with sea lions,
who chase striped bass up the channel,
hoping to feast.
As I walk down outside stairs,
I arrive at my den, welcomed
by my rocking chair, lamp and books.

My authors were rescued from used book stores
or from discard boxes at libraries short of cash.
Orphans from another century, gathered with newborns,
collected in one room on long shelves.
My books are ordered by design
to live with those that share interests.
Lowell's *Poems* near *Nine Horses* by Billy Collins.
Vachel Lindsay's *Collected Poems* by Sara Teasdale,
and John Milton is still speaking to Robert Duncan.

Philosophers and poets wrote of heaven
while novelists and historians spoke of war.
Stacked side by side with other authors
they might have read when they were young,
books and their writers have found a home.

How could anyone burn a book?
These printed words have feelings
that reach out to eager eyes and hearts.
Memories of the past will endure
until words age and crumble
into piles of wind blown ashes.

MEETING A VET ON A RAINY DAY IN HOMER

We were both in a light rain in Homer
while waiting for the cafe to open
when I noticed the visor cap he was wearing
was covered with golden engravings.

His cap said: Marine Corps.
The bill read: WWII, Korea, Vietnam.

He seemed sad and told me that
yesterday, he became the last survivor
of the twenty 16-year-old Iowa farm boys
who left the hay in the barns
and joined the Marines in 1942.

He stayed military instead of milking cows,
led men, not sheep for 30 years.
He dodged bullets instead of mosquitoes
and retired to his Iowa farm.

His buddy, buried here in Homer,
sailed with him on the ships preparing
to invade Japan when suddenly,
there was a fire-bomb destruction
of a city with civilians and children.
It ended the war in the Pacific.

The entire world wept a tear
of compassion for the innocent dead
and for the terrible weapon displayed.
The next day, anchors were raised
and the fleets returned to their home ports.

WHAT THE THUNDER SAID

Title from The Waste Land, by T. S. Eliot

Bats with baby faces upside down,
beat wings, singing out from dripping walls.

Blind at night but swiftly returning at dawn,
filled with insects, chirping out from empty walls.

Sun finds no bats darting from their home,
now asleep in even rows, sighing out from furry walls.

Bugs free to dry and fly alone, but some
gather near a row of bells, silent bats on a wall.

Crepuscular, the merge from day will come
full to dusk, awakening bats on the walls.

Night feeding a swirl but silent as a lamb,
as bats flutter, form and flee the empty walls.

Your servant, David, stands still and dumb,
in awe of nature's feeding plan, within the walls.

AFTERTHOUGHT

What was Helen thinking
as Queen of Menelaos,
flirting and drinking
with the Prince of Troy?

Since I can't envision
a face worth a thousand ships,
I only saw this vision
in my restless slumbers.

As Queen of Sparta,
she led a privileged life.
It was a mistake
to mess with a man without a wife.

Aphrodite had promised Paris
the most beautiful woman alive.
As a guest in the King's Palace,
he should have eyed maidens on the sly.

Instead, he found a beautiful face,
overlooking the ring on her hand.
Soon they're at sea in a race
to reach Troy before pursuing Achaians.

A battle went on for years,
men slaughtered and burned,
because a young man appeared
in front of a young woman who yearned.

Shadows silently slipping as Gods
fought over armies deciding
which chess pieces to move next.
Who was bad, who good?
Their divine board game
had no relation to the morality of man
but served to pass time on Mt. Olympus.

Paris and Helen slept apart
since she was a phantom searching
for Achilles between pyramids in Giza.
Paris and his brothers had other wars to fight
and when the last tale was told,
there weren't any children to pass it on.

PHOENIX

THE MARRIAGE PEARL

My Grandmother's pearl earring,
now set onto a golden band
was hers as a little girl,
then placed on her wedding finger.

The pearl was revered in Swedish lore,
a symbol of the spirit that binds,
a gift of God from the ocean's floor,
handed down from woman to child.

That pearl went with generations
over the ocean to the new land,
now a shadowed display on a shelf —
forgotten, unclaimed, unloved.

Today, wedding plans demand
a new and gaudy diamond
that will stay with the bride
when marital vows are broken.

Like the pearl from the sea,
marriage should be forever.
Honor the words you spoke once:
"Till death do us part, I'll be yours."

BURIAL

In ashes deep
within mangrove bushes,
a small femur bone
of a child, about two,
with other white charred parts
scattered.

Fragments of skull,
a small mandible
without large incisors,
away from the tidal shoreline,
ceremonial
resting in solitude.

The atoll of Fakarava
in the Tahitian chain
is a narrow circular strip
of coral and jungle
separating lagoon from ocean.
Original inhabitants
came by canoe,
sacrificing their dead
to a local deity.

Small offerings
inside a ring
of smooth stones
for many years waiting
to speak to us.

MORGUE REPORT

John Doe was a floater,
cause of death blunt trauma
to the cranium; then tossed
into warm waters below the bridge.

The 20 pound weight attached to his belt
made certain he sank.

His body was attacked
by micro-organisms from within,
as each tiny cell added CO_2
to form tiny bubbles.
The sum effect of this incubation
was the gas volume soon exceeded
the mass of clothes, muscle and weight,
which trapped him on the river's bed.

Once inflated, he elevated
from the dark depths to the surface,
was snagged by a fishing net,
brought to boat, measured
and tossed to cops.

The stench preceded the bloat
on the aluminum gurney
to the thick steel doors
which harbored chilled remains.

The dead reside under vinyl sheets
with an identifying tag on the hallux.
If an autopsy is performed,
body parts are bagged and sealed,

then sent to a mortuary,
where they are coffined or cremated,
and finally returned to ground.

John Doe suffered a fatal blow
but his blood showed heroin.
His brain was typical for Wernickes,
after years of Jim Beam.
His heart had clogged arteries,
his liver as cirrhotic as his brain was wet.
His kidneys were nephrosclerotic,
shrunken to half normal size.

    The Obituary read:
A white male has been identified as
Samuel Anderson Sherlock from Alabama,
who died last month and has been cremated.
He leaves no friends, wives or children,
was never employed and led a hard life.
He died at the age of 42, having gone missing.
The lead weight was never mentioned.
He must have owed someone money.

PHOENIX

"We learn tomorrow from today's ashes."
—Frances Mayes

If we were to build
a new house every day
and it burned
to the ground at night,
what would we learn?

We might learn:

> never to leave a lighted candle unattended
> never to store gasoline under the bed
> never to turn the oven on without a pilot light
> never to plug a Christmas tree into a frayed cord
> never to smoke, especially in bed.

Standing near the ash pile the next morning, we might say:

> the Halsted boys were playing with matches
> PGE linemen must have left a generator on
> my spouse probably left the iron on again
> the fire department was slow to respond
> batteries in the smoke detector were bad.

Perhaps you built your house

> over a smoldering garbage dump
> near a peat bog
> close to an open pit barbeque
> with wood that was too old and dry
> or covered with combustible glue
> near a lot in dispute with an angry neighbor.

Never let the burnt remains
of yesterday's fire blow into today.
Joan D'Arc's ashes flew
with the evening's wind.
The Twin Towers spread toxic fumes
as they sank into their own pit.

Despite the Biblical threat
about returning ashes,
I feel the best of what we were
will arrive as the Phoenix
from the remains of the past
brings wisdom to the future.

MYSTERIOUS

"because our lives are essentially a mystery"
—Diane Frank

Before you add a book
to an overfilled library's shelf,
subtract an old friend or two.
Carve onto stone the elements
unnecessary in your life
and let go.

My character defects need to fall:
I judge you by your shoes,
proudly flash my Harvard ring,
pick lint off a tennis ball
and chide if you are two minutes late.

Planning on visiting the gym more often?
Give up an hour of sleep.
If you're intent on reading *War and Peace*,
leave the funny papers to the kids.
To make a six-month trek to Tibet,
say goodbye to your daily job.

To learn Homeric Greek,
answer the phone without English.
If you want to explore the Arctic,
make certain you leave a will.

It's easy to discard clothes
which haven't fit for years.
The mysterious part is that we hoard.
By stuffing our lives with such a load,
we remain stuck in the old neighborhood.

HEAVENLY DAY

Through vaporous haze rising
from the hot tub shared with neighbors,
I feel suspended in my favorite medium
as if descending gently to 100 feet
in perfect ocean layers,
self contained, in a womb,
without connection to another heart.
I sense the warmth invading
many of my arthritic joints which
open their door to healing.

Transported under the full moon rising
on a windless, crisp January night,
I drift to sleep in my blue reclining chair.
Like the sea, my blanket is blue,
snuggled around two 12-pound
elderly but frisky Bichons Frises
who love me.

Dear God, if heaven is better than this,
I will gladly apply to be a cherub.
My vision and hearing are receding,
but I sense Your Presence anywhere
there is a tub, a chair and a dog.

PARALLEL LIVES

A narrow beach separates
mallards on the bay
foraging for food, mating for life,
migrating when it gets cold,
from the house on the hill
overlooking the beach
inhabited by humans
who neither fly nor swim well.

In Genesis, Moses says
God created every winged bird,
followed by man and woman.
Man was given dominion over birds,
which are fun to kill and tasty to eat.
Birds, however, rule the sky
and give humans inspiration.

In the world of ducks, life is easy.
In the lagoon they paddle,
dive and scrape the ample bottom for food.
Ducks can nest in the grass, birth their young
without fear of predators, and only worry
about buckshot when it turns chilly.

Humans have forgotten how to forage
and live off the land they were given.
They must travel by car, boat or plane
and can't watch TV without a remote.
However, there is no open season on them.

Ducks enjoy and thrive on water
eating and paddling,
watching their ducklings grow until the day
they fly and never return.

Up the hill
human parents toil
well past 65, if they're lucky.
When their children grow, get hungry or bored,
they return home and expect the nest waiting.

ARE ALL SEVENS EQUAL?

"Son todos los sietes iguales?
                —Pablo Neruda: *El Libro de las Prequntas*

Men have a burdensome organ,
walnut sized but not banana shaped.
It enlarges as we age, grows like ears,
noses and girth, and can cause discomfort
when it squeezes as it pleases
the prostatic portion of the urethra.

The prostate specific antigen, the PSA,
is a laboratory reminder of possible cancer
and as wives have to undergo annual exams,
the husbands need a yearly assay
as well as a digital rectal exam, the DRE.

To detect cancerous changes
if the PSA rises or the DRE is abnormal,
large bore needles are plunged deeply
into the gland, and cores of flesh retrieved.
Offending cells will be classified
dictating what therapy is necessary.

The numbers from 2 to 5 are used
and scores vary from 4 to 10 as
2 different samples are analyzed
and the scores totaled signify disease.

You can be happy with a $3 + 4 = 7$
but sad with a result of $4 + 3 = 7$
as not all sevens are equal.
No $2 + 2 = 4$ gland is biopsied.
Only corpses are $5 + 5 = 10$.

Being 7 is acceptable
as long as the first number is 3.

One 7 will have brachytherapy and go home
that day with radioactive seeds and a sore bottom.
The other 7 will have surgery on his pelvic floor
as the walnut-sized gland is ripped from its bed
and nerves and tissues are shredded.
Recovery from surgery will leave
his urinary flow a dribble
and his former manhood reduced
to a noun with the adjective: shriveled.

My father was a 5 + 5 and died.
I was a 3 + 3 and survived.
I hate sitting in Seat 27A on a plane
if a large person is on the aisle seat
blocking my occasional hasty exit.

ODE TO AN ICE POND

Summer's heat has folded into fall,
leaves have shaken loose
onto the pond's glassy sheen.

Fish below don't know
it's getting colder and darker.
Like magic, the top layer clouds
at the edges and freezes over.

Molecules of dihydro-oxygen
bounce, then cling to each other
in an embrace lasting to spring.
Small boys with last year's skates
test their toughness each day.

Cracks and fissures spread
like snakes released from a box
going and coming and scattering skaters
who race to the nearest shore.

Eager the young lads
who want to hasten
the freezing of the pond
so they can fly like birds,
but they must first wait for the freeze
or they will sink like a fish.

A. C.

Air conditioning went off,
people melted into puddles
unaccustomed to searing heat.
Perspiration appeared on foreheads
like morning dew on lilacs
which had already ceased to bloom.

The portable radio blared,
only aware of human discomfort.
Nursing Home patients dropped,
first their dentures, then their spoons.
Schools were closed, kids sent home
to swelter on the airless back porch.

It's not the same as losing juice in winter
when you might freeze to death,
having locked woolen blankets
in boxes in the attic, next to metal
ornaments and trees, buried by
unopened Christmas gifts.

The President's committee on disasters
decided every family must be equipped
with the means to be comfortable
living outdoors for at least 10 days,
in case something worse than hot or cold
such as floods and tornados occur.

In the 50's families built bomb shelters
as protection against the Russians,
but never used since never bombed,
they became expensive storage bins.
In the 60's we packed for the earthquake
which never reduced our towns to rubble.
If a ten foot tsunami comes ashore,
we'd better know how to swim.

Mormons store a year's worth of provisions,
probably rotting in Salt Lake City pantries.
Rambo types stockpile bullets
in case invaded by Eskimos.

It's never a problem to be prepared
but healthy paranoia may go too far.
You don't have to wear a condom
to buy a beer at a gay bar.

THE LONG AND SHORT OF IT

FIRE DANCE

In the boreal forest of Minnesota,
I was 12 years old and frightened.
Every shadow was an Indian brave,
clutching a tomahawk, smearing on
war paint, sprouting feathers.
Images I read last night by flashlight,
tucked in my Sears-Roebuck sleeping bag,
kept me awake until dawn.

.

After four summers, living in tents
with Boy Scout buddies,
grown in stature, wisdom and bravery,
and adorned with itchy peach-fuzz whiskers,
I was picked to do the Fire Dance.
This was done every year for visiting parents
come to reclaim their no longer little boys
at the final campfire ceremony.

Each of nine campers was brightly decked
with feathers and coated with cocoa powder.
Eight carried two long torches the leader lit.
We danced around compass points and then
the leader leapt through a blazing fire
as the tom-toms were silenced.

At 16 I was honored to perform
the Fire Dance indoors
to a packed crowd with real fire.
I suspected the Fire Marshalls were bribed.

I was late for gym class the next day.
Classmates at my stuffy school
had read the morning paper and seen
me on parade in loin cloth and feathers.
They chided me by whooping and laughing.

My secret life as a Boy Scout was exposed,
but I thought less of my friends for this display,
and more of the Blackfeet Indians,
who once performed this dance to fire
to welcome fall into the circle of seasons
as smoke sent their prayers to heaven.

THE LONG AND SHORT OF IT

What didn't count:
Your college freshman grade in Inorganic Chemistry
Your college sophomore grade in second year Calculus.

What mattered was:
You passed all your college classes
You changed your major to Economics
You finished with a BA and a BS
You went to Medical School.

What didn't count:
That you couldn't see the colors in Histology
The gross bodies in jars of formaldehyde
The endless night calls and blood draws
The unhappy bride and marriage.

What mattered was:
You found the beauty between healing and disease
You mastered physical diagnosis and acid-base
That you learned to live and function on little sleep
The right internship program matched you.

What didn't count:
A notice from the President drafting you
How you felt about Vietnam
How you felt about career navy doctors
That your first marriage dissolved.

What mattered was:
You didn't get shot or fall overboard
You finished 10 years of medical training
You found a state, a job, a wife with a child
You made it to forty alive and well
You finally got a dog.

What didn't count:
The size of your bank account
The size of your house
The brand of car you drove
The clothes you wore.

What does matter is:
You did a good job as a physician
You did a good job as an administrator
You never died of three annoying malignancies
You made it to three-score and ten and four more
You found church, A.A., and God
You sleep well but only need five hours
You left the ICU before they told you to
You have two dogs
You are still married
You have a grown daughter
You closed the door on painful past events.

ARS POETICA

Writing a poem
requires cleansing
of body, mind and soul
with careful placement of the trio
in a neat and tidy room.

Then poet poised
over lined paper
expects words to appear
directly from the heart
down arm to pen.

My poems are personal.
My images drip
from a curious eye
on the human condition.

Once printed
then edited
with all spelling
and punctuation
properly intact,
the poet may undress
and dance naked in public.

MOTHER

I remember a river-mouth
with rains recently open,
letting steelhead trout move
from salt to fresh water.

Synapses of that small brain
sent her on an LSD trip.
Flashes of home, of being young,
now laden with eggs, returning.

She swallowed my berry of roe,
hooked herself deeply,
fought current and her large belly,
landed on the slope of the shore.

But, not done, lidless eyes fixed,
gills barely moving, still alive,
she made it perfectly clear:

"This is my river and I have work to do.
You've had your fun, now let me go."
I couldn't argue with such a Queen.
Our natures melded; she swam upstream.

BULL RIDER AT THE VICTORY

I drove north on 35E from Minneapolis
and stopped at Old State Highway 61,
where Andrew at the Victory Service Station,
works the night shift selling coffee and gas.

Here in the heart
of Minnesota farmland
settled late in the 19th century
by immigrants from Sweden,
my grandfather's farm,
one of the originals after the Hinckley fire,
has unplowed fields, an empty barn,
with an unused pig sty nearby.

Andrew is 22, six feet tall and lanky.
He rides bulls on the rodeo circuit
and this past weekend was thrown four times.
This wasn't his first concussion
and, "not a bad one," he said in a drawl
common to the area where
hordes of penniless farmers
dug in roots and stayed.

Andrew shrugged off his recent injury,
told me it was number 24.
He claimed eight fractured ribs,
which go with the territory.

His 12-year-old brother wants in
to the glory and pain of the rodeo,
"but he doesn't have the passion
to do this over and over."

Rewards are few
but the beer is free
as long as you sign autographs
for starry-eyed teenage girls
in short Levi skirts.

AVALON COVE

Gentle waves break
on the concrete wall near the ferries
overlooking the cove at Avalon
on Catalina Island,
26 miles from San Pedro Harbor.

The water is murky,
shimmering with diesel fuel
and only the occasional
small black crab crawling
on shore rocks, hinting of life below.

Once I plunged 100 feet
within view of this shore
into caves around coral heads.
I chased lobsters, petted abalone,
spied a small octopus clutching
a smaller grouper who was losing
the battle between creatures
that call the ocean home.

I heard a four-year-old's happy note:
"Look, Dad, the ocean!"
as the glazed eyes of tourists
scanning the horizon saw only
the top of the hidden kingdom.

COUNTRY HORSES AND CITY DOGS

My cousin's four Belgian horses
finished their ration of oats
and were munching on the hay mound,
pulling green tufts into their grinding molars.
Their horse chow was in the middle of a flat field
and they were sharing horse gossip
about recent storms and wolf sightings
when I whistled and called.

They barely lifted their heads
away from their lunch,
repulsed that a two-legged stranger
would interrupt their chewing.
I got the stare and an occasional snort,
but they didn't come running
like my dogs do at home.

My Bichons Frises can't pull a sleigh
or live outdoors in winter.
They need their kibble scooped
and freshened with chicken parts.
They love the warmth of the communal bed
and never need new iron shoes.

THERE WAS A TIME

When I am vexed by a toilet
that doesn't flush or overflows,
I reach for the plumber's helper
or pretend I am standing in line in winter
with a 4-year-old who will be my auntie
and her six other young,
restless, agitated siblings
waiting for two brothers
behind a locked door
of the two-holer latrine
west of the farm house.
Hoping they are not lingering,
tearing the softer pages from
last fall's Sears-Roebuck Catalogue,
the girl who will be my mother
says aloud: "Get on with business,
open the door, scoop up an armload
of kindling I just splintered from the log,
and tell Mom we'll be in soon for breakfast."

BUCK

My two aging Bichons Frises
insist on sharing my blue leather recliner,
but allowing me to sit first, spread the blanket
and prepare for a two animal leap
into security and heaven.

My Grandfather, on the other hand,
permitted only one dog at a time
to be the farm beast who guarded the house,
herded the cows, confronted gophers,
chased foxes and ate the milk filter
freshly curdled with cream.
He had freedom to roam
60 acres of hills, fields and forest.

Each dog shared relatives
and all had the same name.
They were German Shepherds
and gentle as lambs with children.
Facial scars, blinded eyes, missing limbs,
spoke silently of fight with wolves.
No Buck was ever allowed indoors
except to the milking shed for his treat.
None ever cuddled in an easy chair
or slept with parents in their bed.

MOOSE IN ALASKA

It was not a chance encounter,
as I was in her neighborhood
which once was swamp, not a tarred road.
The mother moose had a calf to feed
so she had to find lilies floating,
since they couldn't grow through tar.
She looked at me with hunger, anger
and curiosity through big brown eyes.
I moved first, she didn't follow.

SMELLS OF AUTUMN

Ice freezing and thawing,
sweat sox damp
inside leather skate boots,
the slow accustomed odor
of my unwashed T-shirt
that freezes and melts daily,
never taken home
during hockey season.
Home after practice,
my chore is to clear the walks
so people and cars can safely exit.
I know every crack in the concrete
and where to throw each shovel of snow.

Crisp air,
that burrows through my nostrils
and freezes my tongue
despite a scarf over my nose.

The frozen breath
of my high school girlfriend
lightly tinted with Sen-Sen
and the chilly cloud
she leaves in her wake
as she blows me a frozen kiss.

Wet slush dripping off overshoes
comingling in the cloak room
with the drying scarves at the end
of a grade school classroom.

A hint of caramel candy
on the lips of my teacher
as I lean over my exam paper.

I used to smell whole neighborhoods
filled with smoke from piles of
burning birch and maple leaves.

Where do the dead leaves go now
so they can burn and smell so good?

ABOUT THE AUTHOR

David Connor is a retired physician living in San Rafael, California, with his wife and two dogs. His interest in poetry began early in life, influenced by his mother and a great aunt, a poet of the 1930's. He did not have a literary education; instead he graduated from Harvard University with a B.A. in Economics and from the University of Minnesota with a B.S. and an M.D. He practiced Nephrology in the San Francisco Bay Area for 30 years and began attending poetry workshops with Diane Frank, Dale Biron, and Prartho Sereno. He still practices medicine in Northern California, as long as the doctors he covers for are near fly fishing rivers.

PRAISE FOR
THE LONG AND SHORT OF IT
by David Connor

"David Connor's gutsy collection of poetic renderings is a compendium of the 20th century American life as seen through the unflinching eye of a dedicated physician and investigator into the mysteries of body and soul. In poems that are quirky, specific, and complex — layered with horrors, humor, and redemption — we find images so clear they become mirrors, and we are able to glimpse, for a moment, our own invaluable inexplicable lives."
>—Prartho Sereno, Author of *Call from Paris*; and *Causing a Stir,*
>*The Secret Lives & Loves of Kitchen Utensils.*

"*The Long and Short of It* is a book of wit and wisdom, a life of experience distilled into vision and joy."
>—Diane Frank, Author of *Yoga of the Impossible,*
>*Blackberries in the Dream House*, and *Swan Light.*

"From growing up country in Minnesota, to facing sad, brave and freely offered death, as the physician who makes it legal, David Connor's poems heal grief with compassion and sutures, discover beauty between healing and disease, and laugh in the rolling of the unexpected world he discovers. He offers to us, as his traveling companions, his take on historical figures, philosophy, and survivorship on planet earth."
>—Melissa Hobbs, Author of *Under the Pomegranate Sun.*

"I like many kinds of poems. But most of all, I like poems that jostle and surprise me. I like poems that have bonuses and that snap me into a kind of heightened attention. David writes this kind of poem. The kind I wholeheartedly recommend!"
>—Dale Biron, Author of *Why We Do Our Daily Practices.*

www.ingramcontent.com/pod-product-compliance
Lightning Source LLC
Chambersburg PA
CBHW022033090426
42741CB00007B/1043